ONE CHRIST
ONE BODY
JESUS IS LORD

Donald William Sanders

XULON PRESS

Xulon Press
2301 Lucien Way #415
Maitland, FL 32751
407.339.4217
www.xulonpress.com

Paperback ISBN-13: 978-1-66285-929-8
Hard Cover ISBN-13: 978-1-66285-930-4
Ebook ISBN-13: 978-1-66285-931-1

PREFACE

As sure as we are born of man, we are born into sin. God's word assures us that from birth, we are in a **war** *"against principalities, against powers, against rulers of the darkness of this world, and spiritual wickedness in high places"* (Ephesians 6:12). I believe that many Christians do not understand that we are all participating in spiritual warfare each day of our lives.

God has given humanity "free will"; therefore, we have the right to choose our destiny. As we grow into life, that same God-given "free will" not only allows but, in and of itself, demands that we accept responsibility for our own soul's salvation. There is no "will" involved as to whether you want to be in the fight or not; you were born into it. The free will aspect comes regarding how you choose to manage the life given to you. It would be best to decide the direction in which you will move in your life upon reaching the age of understanding. What does a man profit if he gains the entire world and loses his soul? Or what shall a man give in exchange for his soul?

Jesus said, *"Let the children alone, and do not hinder them from coming to Me; for the kingdom of heaven belongs to such as these"* (Matthew 19:14).

We were all children at one point in our lives, so Jesus's statement in this scripture is "all-inclusive." Being born again enables us to receive the ultimate power of the Holy Spirit, who will enter and dwell in each of us, to teach and guide us in the footsteps of righteousness. Jesus' sacrifice on the cross was payment for the sins of all humanity, and once we accept Him as our Lord and Savior, we become the righteousness of God.

I believe God calls not only individuals but also families; therefore, we are all called to serve a King. That King is the "King of Kings" and the only bridge covering the sin gap between God and man. His name is Jesus. You can rest assured that if you choose to make Jesus your Lord and Savior, you are "chosen" because you answered the call from God himself and will receive His Holy Spirit, making you "more than a conqueror" and under the direct authority of the Highest. God provides us with our weapons of warfare and victory over sin in our lives. The weapons He provides are found throughout the Bible and **must** be loaded with the proper ammunition, which is ... **faith**. Nothing can work without it. We've been chosen to fight the good fight of faith against an enemy that comes to kill, steal, and destroy... THIS MEANS WAR.

> *May the LORD bless and keep you; the LORD make his face shine on you and be gracious to you; the LORD turn his face toward you and give you peace. –*
>
> **Numbers 6:24-26 NIV**

One Christ One Body; Jesus is Lord

Having received Jesus as our Lord and Savior, we are believers in the Body of Christ. This means the whole body of Christ as it spans in its entirety from the north to the south and from the east to the west. Our goal is to demonstrate and promote a lifestyle that allows our light to shine so that others might see our good works and glorify our God in Heaven.

The "church is the church" no matter where it's located. The many members worldwide comprise "The Body of Christ" and are not limited to the various denominations designated by humanity. The only condition that makes us whole is that we truly accept Jesus as our Lord and Savior. Although denominations can define specific disciplines within the Body of Christ, there will always be One Christ, One Body, and Jesus will always be the King of Kings and the Lord of Lords for that Body.

Contrary to what many believe and or have believed over our lifetimes, God is in control. As the Supreme Almighty Being who has given life to the very existence of all things and every being, we are indebted to His desire and life's expectancies.

*"**The God who made the world and everything in it is the Lord of heaven and earth** and does not live in temples built by hands. And he is not served by human hands as if he needed anything because he gives all men life, breath, and everything else." He made all the nations from one man that they should inhabit the whole earth; and the boundaries of their lands. God did this so they would seek and perhaps reach out for Him and find him, though He is not far from us. "For in Him we live and move and have our being." As some of your own have said, "We are His offspring." Acts 17:24-28 NIV*

TABLE OF CONTENTS

Chapter 1

WHY ARE WE HERE?

God created man in the book of Genesis after creating a place for our existence and survival. He didn't just make us; according to Genesis Chapter 1:26-27, God created us in His image.

Then God said, *"Let Us make man in Our image, according to Our likeness; and let them rule over the fish of the sea and the birds of the sky and the cattle and all the earth, and over every creeping thing that creeps on the earth."* God created man in His image, in the image of God, He created him; male and female, He created them.

I would say that makes us His offspring. We are the children of God. Therefore, like any parent, there is an expectation of how their children's life should be with a defining purpose and expectation. Those purposes and expectations are first revealed because God made us in His image. He expects us to be like Him.

The point is we are all the children of God; and, as such, we are obligated to be obedient to His word. The scripture says that obedience is better than sacrifice. I agree with that, and I know that when we comply and obey God's word, He remains in control of all that happens in our lives. Being the "just" God that He is, we have been given the right to decide our destinies. God will not force Himself on us. His word allows each one to be responsible for his own soul's salvation; therefore, the choice is ours with God's recommendation to choose life through Him. The following scripture demonstrates what I will refer to as "His offer."

> **Deuteronomy 30:19-20** *"I call heaven and earth to record this day against you, that I have set before you life and death, blessing and cursing: therefore choose life, that both thou and thy seed may live: That thou mayest love the LORD thy God, and that thou mayest obey his voice, and that thou mayest cleave unto him: for he is thy life, and the length of thy days: that thou mayest dwell in the land which the LORD swore unto thy fathers, to Abraham, to Isaac, and to Jacob, to give them."*

The fact of the matter is that our choices in our lives will be the seeds that we sow. They will bring a harvest, and we will reap from the seeds we sow. You must ask yourself: "Will I choose Heaven or Hell?

Accepting Jesus as your Lord and Savior

God wants everyone to be saved. His word says so, and the following scriptures speak to that desire. The Bible has over a hundred scriptures that confirm this. I will limit myself to what I believe are three of those most compelling scriptures:

> **2 Peter 3:9 — King James Bible** *"The Lord is not slack concerning his promise, as some men count slackness, but is longsuffering to us-ward, not willing that any should perish, but that all should come to repentance."*

> **John 3:16 — King James Bible** *"For God so loved the world, that he gave his only begotten Son, that whosoever believeth in him should not perish, but have everlasting life."*

Romans 8:38-39 — English Standard Version *"For I am sure that neither death nor life, nor angels nor rulers, nor things present nor things to come, nor powers, nor height nor depth, nor anything else in all creation, will be able to separate us from the love of God in Christ Jesus our Lord."*

Chapter 2

THE PURPOSE OF THE CHURCH

Every church receives tithes and offerings because it needs funds to operate. This is accomplished by passing the collection plate, setting a box in the back of the sanctuary, online giving, or other methods. Because the church primarily has responsibilities to its members, surrounding community, and God, how the church uses those funds is highly essential.

First, a church has a responsibility to its members. Remember that this is considered the House of God in proper context and not just a building. It's become our mindset that church is a place to go on Sundays to worship God. The word of God says we are not to forsake the assembling of ourselves together as some do; however, the problem is that we have become so programmed to report to what some consider as a physical building at least once or twice a week that we lose sight of the fact that we aren't just going to church. We are the church. There's no life in the building if we don't come together. It only comes alive with our presence and the presence of God, and when we leave, that spirit that lives inside of us should be going with us to share the gospel with everyone we meet who is willing to receive.

Inside the church building is where dedicated members should be striving to do whatever it takes to reach out and help others. There is a primary responsibility to serve and help others in need within the boundaries of the physical structure. Caring for each other inside the church and contributing to their success changes lives. It will significantly contribute to strengthening the membership within. It could additionally draw new visitors and members from outside the walls of the building as it sends the message that in the eyes of God, helping is a mandatory practice bringing a level of security to believers and other onlookers.

Given that people like to share the good news, after leaving the physical structure, the seeds sown inside should be served to those outside and demonstrate one of the quickest ways to show how Jesus changes lives. Too often, we see a need and wait for the pastor or someone on staff to take responsibility. But that's not the way the church should work. 1 Timothy 5:8 says, "if anyone does not provide for his own, especially for those of his household, he has denied the faith and is worse than an unbeliever." This scripture doesn't just apply to the individual members but the entire church. And to take it a step further, no one escapes the Word of God, whether saved or unsaved.

We have been given skills, abilities, and opportunities to serve. For example, in Timothy's church, the women ran a widows ministry (1 Timothy 5:16), and elders directed church affairs while others were devoted to teaching and preaching (1 Timothy 5:17).

Scripture tells us we are to let our lights shine so that others may see our good works and glorify our Father, which is in Heaven. The church is at its best when people inside the building take Jesus' message outside and serve those they meet.

At one point in the Bible, Jesus turned to His disciples and told them that the harvest was plentiful, but the workers were few. The point was that only a handful of workers were available or willing to go out and gather the harvest, which represented the people. If the church members don't reach out to the spiritually lost, then who will?

During my research, I found that various local churches in the first century also offered to help other churches in need. Specifically, the church in Jerusalem was suffering from persecution and famine, and the church in Antioch provided resources to help (Acts 11:29). Paul later took love gifts from Galatia (1 Corinthians 16:1), Corinth (1 Corinthians

16:3), Macedonia, and Achaia (Romans 15:25–26) to Jerusalem. He was accompanied by emissaries from Berea, Thessalonica, Derbe, and the province of Asia (Acts 20:4).

Second, a church has a responsibility to its surrounding community. Outreach is necessary. *"As we have the opportunity, let us do good to all people, especially those who belong to the family of believers"* (Galatians 6:10). This verse sets the priority—God's family first—but we are also to seek ways to "do good" to everyone. Of course, this must involve evangelism (Acts 1:8). A healthy church should send out missionaries (see Acts 13:2–3) or at least support missionaries in various service fields.

As evidenced by where it spends its money, a church that loses its outward focus shows signs of spiritual weakness. Church consultant and author Thom S. Rainer, in his book *Autopsy of a Dead Church*, states that one of the symptoms of a dying church is that the percentage of the budget for members' needs keeps increasing while the money earmarked for outreach decreases. Is this representative of the church you attend? If you are a member of a Board of Directors or a Pastor who has the sole responsibility of a church, are you measuring up to God's expectations? Read the following scriptures very carefully. Then answer the question that follows.

Malachi 3:7-11 — King James Version

> *"[7] Even from the days of your fathers ye are gone away from mine ordinances and have not kept them. Return unto me, and I will return unto you, saith the LORD of hosts. But ye said Wherein shall we return?*
>
> *[8] Will a man rob God? Yet ye have robbed me. But ye say Wherein have we robbed thee? In tithes and offerings.*

> *9 Ye are cursed with a curse: for ye have robbed me, even this whole nation.*
>
> *10 Bring ye all the tithes into the storehouse, that there may be meat in mine house, and prove me now herewith, saith the LORD of hosts, if I will not open you the windows of heaven, and pour you out a blessing, that there shall not be room enough to receive it.*
>
> *11 And I will rebuke the devourer for your sakes, and he shall not destroy the fruits of your ground; neither shall your vine cast her fruit before the time in the field, saith the LORD of hosts."*

That is from God's lips to our ears. Here's the question to ask yourself; and keep in mind that to whom much is given, much is required.

Question: Are you, who receive God's tithes and offerings, doing the things you are expected to do with those tithes and offerings?

From Paul's perspective, the apostles were instructed to remember the poor. That perspective, according to God's word, should never change. Charitable work to benefit the poor within the church should be included as part of a church's budget. In addition, smaller churches that are known to be suffering, if willing to receive, should be given direction and assistance in developing their ministries to draw more people. The larger churches located near them should review their circumstances and assist within the boundaries of the word of God. After all, does the Word not say; give, and it shall be given to you in good measure, pressed down, shaken together, and running over, shall man give into your bosom? (Luke 6:38).

Do the small churches not represent the Body of Christ as well? I'm sure that God's spiritual law of giving goes beyond blessing the individual giver. It includes churches, groups, businesses, and other organizations giving and receiving is a spiritual law.

As previously stated, a church has a responsibility to God. Our Lord knows His church (Revelation 2:2, 9, 13, 19), and He commands that His Word be preached (; 2 Timothy 4:2) and that "the mystery of Christ" be proclaimed (Colossians 4:3). Delivering the gospel is most important. Anything that furthers that goal should be given priority, and paying the pastor is part of that goal. *"The elders who direct the church's affairs are worthy of double honor, especially those whose work is preaching and teaching. For Scripture says, 'Do not muzzle an ox while it is treading out the grain,' and 'The worker deserves his wages"* (1 Timothy 5:17–18). Those who faithfully minister the Word of God should be realistically compensated for their work as the Shepherd leading the flock (see also 1 Corinthians 9:11).

Wisdom regarding a church's expenditures is necessary, and we should be praying for that wisdom (James 1:5). There is nothing sinful about having a fine building or nicely kept grounds. Still, we sometimes wonder if the money would be better spent supporting another missionary or aiding the poorer churches worldwide.

The church's goal should be to do the work of God in the world. And everything should be done to the glory of God (1 Corinthians 10:31). The early church *"devoted themselves to the apostles' teaching and fellowship, breaking bread and prayer"* (Acts 2:42). Perhaps these actions—spreading the Word, fellowshipping with one another, observing communion, and praying—should be an essential guide to how a church uses its offerings.

Chapter 3

LEARNING TO UNLEARN

Throughout our lives, we are programmed from birth to feel a certain way about who we are, what we are, and why we are; based on where we live, to whom we were exposed, and our environment. In most cases, we become who others think we should be unless we begin to unlearn.

To become the best of who we can be, we must exercise the ability to reduce the influence of old skills and prevent old ideas from affecting our unconscious bias and other cognitive skills. According to the word of God, we are to get wisdom and understanding and not forget His words or swerve from them. We are not to forsake wisdom, as it will protect us. We are instructed to love her, and she will watch over us. Wisdom is supreme and provides us with insight and understanding. Proverbs 4 verses 5 thru 7 (KJV) states it like this: "Get wisdom, get understanding: forget it not; neither decline from the words of my mouth. Forsake her not, and she shall preserve thee: love her, and she shall keep thee. Wisdom is the principal thing; therefore, get wisdom: and with all thy getting get understanding."

To fully benefit from this learning phenomenon, we must first understand the process. When you comprehend the information you've learned, you know it in one form or another. As you continue to understand the learning process and adequately apply it to your decision-making, you exercise and gain wisdom. This circle of communication creates a continuous cycle of understanding and learning. It's a process that should never stop throughout our lives.

An example of unlearning would be something we all do at times. We tend to observe things that others do where we are tempted to criticize. It happens to us all and is a subconscious perception in day-to-day life, having become a learned behavior. No one is perfect, so in that regard, we should teach ourselves not to criticize; but recognize that it would be an excellent time to unlearn. If you can't see a problem, you can't fix it or adequately address it. Don't turn people off; instead, turn them on so they hear and understand rather than become offended, resulting in a closed mind because of negative criticism.

We must also be open-minded, listening for opportunities to understand better who they are and who we are in the process. Proverbs 27:17 teaches us that "iron sharpens iron." It should be universally seen as positive: Wise people should be questioning, encouraging, coaching, and challenging each other. According to the word of God, Hebrews 10:25 KJV; we are to live accordingly, *"Not forsaking the assembling of ourselves together, as the manner of some; but exhorting one another: and so much the more, as ye see the day approaching."*

Getting wisdom will be accompanied by new beginnings. Whether saved or unsaved, everyone should examine themselves regularly. At times (probably often) if we look closely, we will recognize there will be the need for starting certain areas of our lives anew. There is the saying that "old habits die hard." There is probably some truth in that statement, given that we need to unlearn certain areas of our lives; but as we noted before, there is a need to recognize those areas. Once identified, correction is imminent.

How do we change?

I have found that you can't receive what you can't believe in your life. It's one of those things that we know subconsciously; but at the first sign that things might not appear to be going our way, we give up.

However, God says that faith without works is dead. We must realize that any possibility of accomplishment dies when we quit in all our understanding. We have an obligation to ourselves to fight the good fight of faith as each one of us is responsible for our own soul's salvation. One of the many weapons of warfare that God has provided is His infallible word; it can be ignored by choice, but it can't be broken. When you sow it into your spirit, it begins to live inside you. The more understanding you get, the more wisdom you have. The more insight, the more knowledge, and the stronger you become. This is the harvest of gaining increased understanding. Galatians 6 tells us that a man reaps what he sows. Therefore, the one who sows to please his sinful nature, from that nature, will reap destruction; the one who sows to please the Spirit, from the Spirit, will reap eternal life. Let us not become weary in doing good, for we will reap a harvest at the proper time if we do not give up. If you don't believe in the righteousness of God in your life, it's because you made a personal choice not to. I urge you to choose wisely because we are who we think we are. Therefore, a strong emphasis on unlearning is needed. Change is necessary, but only we can do it; it must be a choice followed and supported by our actions.

God honors all who believe and fight the good fight of faith without regard for who you are or what you do.

Scripture tells us that we have all sinned and fallen short of the glory of God (Romans 3:23). Even after accepting Jesus as Lord and Savior, we still sin. Of course, it's (in most cases) not with intent.

However, as we continue through life, there is always the process of learning and unlearning. That is part of the process where God instructs us to get wisdom and, in all our getting, to get understanding. Does the Apostle Paul ask if we should continue in sin because of that fact? The answer is a resounding "NO." The desire to continue in sin would be a total misunderstanding of God's grace and a demonstration of (whether intentional or unintentional) contempt for the sacrifice of Jesus on the cross. Just as Christ died to sin, we are to resist sin day by day, and this is the new life we are to live. But the Christian life is not simply a matter of refusing sin or playing dead to it. We are supposed to be alive to God as we live in Christ Jesus, and our desire to live for Him should be very much active in us. The forgiveness of sins brings the Holy Spirit and reconciles us back to God. It's what makes it possible for us to inherit eternal life. If a man has all the wealth in the world, but his sins are not forgiven, he will remain a man who is lost.

When I reflect on my own life, I can say that it was only through the actions of a praying grandmother that I was able to get through my childhood years. As I grew up, I lived in a two-bedroom household consisting of my grandmother, mother, two uncles, one aunt, and six of us children. I grew up thinking that was normal and everybody had the same lifestyle. My father existed but wasn't a part of our lives, and we rarely even saw him unless we went to a club called the American Legion, which was a couple of blocks from our home. We were raised by our mother, who our grandmother consistently coached. Although our father rarely showed his face during those times, I didn't miss him because he didn't have an actual presence in my life.

I can remember my grandmother praying, what seemed like forever, all the time. Every day she would pull out the giant family Bible and read it until she fell asleep in her chair with the Bible open on her lap. She would attend what we commonly referred to as a "holiness church" on weekends. And, during the week, it was church services, what seemed like every day. I can't say that we were made to go to church because I don't remember whether it was optional. I just know I was there. I watched as my grandmother and other church members would speak in tongues and dance in the spirit. Even though I had absolutely no hint of understanding of what was going on until later in life, I enjoyed the services. Before attending the holiness church, I remember attending Sunday school at a Baptist church where I learned nothing because of my youth. Most of the services I heard seemed like nothing more than babysitting services while the adults were being taught.

My mother would never allow us to speak ill of our father or even point out things we felt were wrong as we grew through the ages. Neither she nor my grandmother would say anything negative regarding him or the stuff he did or didn't do. Absent being taught in some areas about life, I was learning through others from exposure by comparing my life to those around me. I knew right from wrong in most cases, but not as much as I should have. This is why, especially for me, there exists a need for the process of learning to unlearn.

As for my mother, we, her children, seem to be her job. She was a "stay at home" mother, and I can't begin to talk about everything I learned from her. She made it her business to teach us all she knew, especially me as the oldest son. I learned to wash dishes at such an early age that I had to stand on a stool to reach the sink. An incident that came to mind, back then, was that one day while washing the dishes I saw my older sister's toy iron sitting on the sink. I plugged it in and decided to iron the water. The electric shock that came from sticking the iron into the water was so hard; that it knocked me off the stool that I was standing on and kept me from being electrocuted. I didn't know it then, but I believe God kept me alive that day. I was about six years old at the time. It would be one of the first times I can remember when I experienced the grace of God, and it wouldn't be the last.

There were things I learned to do from my mother that I never realized a woman could do during those days. This was because of the way society thought about things. There was man's work, and then there was woman's work, and neither of the two paths should ever cross. My mother taught me how to repair plumbing and to crawl under the house and wrap the pipes to keep them from freezing during the winter months. She taught me how to do electrical work, including changing the igniters on floor furnaces, how to make the paste to hang wallpaper with an undetectable seam, to rebuild porches, repair roofs and build fencing, make clothing from scratch as well as a host of other skills. Today, she was what we might call a "Jack of All Trades." All of these things she taught; I knew very well by the time I was a teenager. During those years, I learned that anything a man could do, so could a woman. Not to mention, she could do some things even better. These were things I never forgot. However, that part of learning to unlearn had value for me; it wasn't the same for many of my friends and associates during that generation because "men were men" and "women were women," and each had their place. In Proverbs 31 we see the true definition as God demonstrates the characteristics of a great woman. I affectionately liken that description to my own mother over the years. A great woman is not restricted to just being a mother, but a working woman as well. She's a woman with dignity and worthy of honor. I once read that a Proverbs 31 Woman is a woman who pursues God's wisdom instead of the world's wisdom. She's not concerned with what seems right according to the world. Instead, she focuses on God's truth. Her biggest desire is to honor Him.

Learning to unlearn is an invaluable lesson for the world we live in today. However, we must keep God at the helm during the learning and unlearning process because we can veer off the path of righteousness without Him to guide us.

Chapter 4

FORGIVENESS

What does God say about forgiveness?

> *"And when you stand praying, if you hold anything against anyone, forgive them, so that your Father in heaven may forgive you your sins." Mark 11:25 NIV*

> *"Blessed is the one whose transgressions are forgiven, whose sins are covered." Psalm 32:1 NIV*

Just as God has forgiven our sins against Him, we are to forgive the sins of others against us. Is it an easy thing to do? No, but it does make it right. Even in the face of those sins that have been committed against us, forgiveness tends to fall in last place. When we cannot forgive, it is just another choice that we have made of our own volition. When it comes to forgiveness, many of us are self-centered. It is easier to receive forgiveness than to give it. One of the considerations of being on the receiving end of forgiveness is that the receiver is the one who has usually caused hurt to another. When the circumstances have been reversed, let us face it, being forgiven is much easier than forgiving.

We must realize that there will always be consequences for our actions in life itself. This "right to choose" comes with consequences for our decisions. In most cases, those decisions determine what direction our lives will take from there. When you fail to forgive others, it locks you into a place of unforgiveness until you do. If you could, picture yourself standing before our Almighty God, who has forgiven every sin you have committed in your lifetime, explaining why He should permit you to enter the gates of Heaven after you refuse to forgive those who have sinned against you.

In talking about unforgiveness, I have to reflect on my history. Earlier I mentioned that my mother would never allow us to speak badly about our father, who was never around. That is true, and she demanded that we always honor him as our father because the Bible says that we should always give honor to our mothers and fathers so that our Father in heaven would honor us. Those were never her exact words, but because of our home environment and the fact that my grandmother was always saying, "God don't like ugly," we could never be truly open about the way we felt on the inside. None of us wanted to go to hell, but that was always an underlying fear to help us stay in check. As I grew older, my experiences with an absentee father were incredibly challenging. Things that I would be exposed to, like my father dating girls closer to my age than his and knowing that they were better dressed than me and my siblings in our hand-me-downs and clothes with patches to cover the holes, were something that cut deep and caused scarring on the inside. We lived on welfare, and I had to leave school once a month to collect the welfare baskets from the county so our family could eat. It seemed like I was the only one and living in a small town did not help because everyone knew everyone's business. Since my mother did not drive or have a driver's license, it was me and my little wagon that made the trip each month for the food baskets. It was years later that I learned that we were not the only family on welfare because I never saw any of my fellow students at the food bank. I did see some of their parents; however, I recognized them from looking back to past visits and remembering familiar faces. Episodes like this created an extreme dislike inside me for my father, even though I was taught to love and respect him regardless.

At sixteen, I remember one of my younger brothers was at a nearby playground. I was playing basketball with some friends when I saw my father with his hands around my brother's neck. It looked like he was choking him, so I yelled for him to stop. When he did not, the only thing I could think to do was yell at him from the top of my lungs and call him a dirty name. He immediately let go and came after me. My father had previously done some time in prison and was built with an Arnold Schwarzenegger kind of body, so I ran and jumped over a chain-linked fence. When I landed, my foot came down on a piece of wood shaped like a 2X4 with one end rotted off like a handle. As my father attempted to jump the fence after me, I picked up the piece of wood and struck him over the head with it. I was so scared that I took off running and it felt as if I was home, two blocks away, before he hit the ground. As I was explaining to my mother what happened, an ambulance went racing by the house, and at the same time, my mother received a phone call saying that my father was bleeding from his head and was in an ambulance on the way to the hospital. The fear of him dying because of what I had done scared my mother and me. She immediately got on the phone and called my aunt, who was living in Indianapolis, Indiana, to see if I could come to say with her. There was a fear for both of us that he might die from the injury I had caused. Fortunately, we were told that he was all right within the next few hours, so I did not have to leave.

The next day, I was playing basketball again when I felt this tight grip on my arm. I looked around to see my father and immediately thought he would end me at once. Instead, he looked me in the eyes and said he was glad to know that I could take care of myself and assured me that I did not have to worry about him bothering us again. I later found out that he had to have eight stitches to close the wound on his head. Although relieved, I went home and shook like a leaf for the next few hours. Over time, we became friends. We never had what I considered a father and son relationship, but it turned out to be more respectful. I not only had to learn to forgive him for not being what I thought would have been a good father, but I had to forgive myself for hitting him over the head with the board. It was wrong, and I knew it; but it seemed like there was no other alternative at the time. Turning my life over to Jesus Christ and learning that God orders the footsteps of the righteous made me feel more like the Lord had intervened in a way that brought peace to both of us. It also helped me understand how important it is to live a life of forgiveness. Even though it is not always us doing the praying, it helps to have someone praying on our behalf. In this case, I believe it was my praying grandmother, and that God was listening.

Taking a closer look at the act of forgiveness from other perspectives can help you understand its importance much better. Here are seven of the many reasons why forgiveness is so important:

1) It is what God wants. The sacrifice of Jesus on the cross is for everyone. His precious blood paid for the sins of the entire world. No exceptions. Who are we not to honor that?

    1) *"If we confess our sins, he is faithful to forgive and cleanse us from all unrighteousness."* (1 John 1:9). If God has forgiven us of our sins and cleansed us of all unrighteousness, should we purposefully reject the work He has done?

    2) Although forgiveness awards the other person, it is for you, the forgiver. It helps keep your heart free and clear of the seeds of unforgiveness.

1) *"Therefore, you have no excuse, O man, every one of you who judges. For in passing judgment on another, you*

condemn yourself because you, the judge, practice the very same things." (Romans 2:1). The question for us: Is this passing judgment a form of unforgiveness?

2) A woman was accused of infidelity, and the people standing around began tempting Jesus to pass judgment against her. As they continued asking him, he lifted himself and said unto them, He that is without sin among you, let him first cast a stone at her. (John 8:7, KJV):

3) Regarding consequences for our actions, recent studies have found that the act of forgiveness can reap huge rewards for your health, lowering the risk of heart attack; improving cholesterol levels and sleep; and reducing pain, blood pressure, anxiety, depression, and stress.

4) *"Be ye holy because I am holy."* (1 Peter 1:16). This is the written word of God. This says it all.

It is plain to see that God is no respecter of persons. He asks that we be holy because He is holy. He asks that we be like Him as much as we can. This cannot happen without putting in the effort. Knowing that we will inevitably fail because we are human, God provides us with an avenue to be forgiven and repent for our sins. Therefore, we must not only ask forgiveness for our sins but also give forgiveness to others.

I have heard people say, not to exclude my own iniquities, that we should forgive but "don't forget." Despite this thought process, the scripture is clear on God's position:

> *"If you forgive other people when they sin against you, your heavenly Father will also forgive you."* (Matthew 6:14). God wants us to forgive and learn to forget as a

learning point. His word says, *"I, even I, am he who blots out your transgressions for my own sake and remembers your sins no more."* (Isaiah 43:25).

In essence, forgive and be forgiven, and then forget:

And Jesus said unto him, *"No man, having put his hand to the plow, and looking back, is fit for the kingdom of God."* (Luke 9:62).

This is specifically worth taking some time to meditate on.

Chapter 5

NEW BEGINNINGS

Accepting Jesus as Lord and Savior does not require starting life over. Instead, it means to begin rebuilding the life God has already given you. Being "born again is a spiritual rebirth of your existing life and how you choose to live it. We are to adjust to a new way of living by letting the "old man" pass away. This would be that part of your life that is not pleasing to God and, in most cases, not even to yourself. To gain more sustenance on this subject matter, let us review Ephesians 4:19 -25. *"Who being past feeling have given themselves over unto lasciviousness, to work all uncleanness with greediness. But ye have not so learned Christ; If so be that ye have heard him, and have been taught by him, as the truth is in Jesus: That ye put off concerning the former conversation the older man, which is corrupt according to the deceitful lusts; And be renewed in the spirit of your mind; And that ye put on the new man, which after God is created in righteousness and true holiness. Wherefore putting away lying, speak every man truth with his neighbor: for we are one of another."*

Changing our lives is about adjusting and readjusting. It is an ongoing process that requires learning who you are, recognizing things you do, and leaving behind any former activities that played a role in corrupting our lives.

After graduating from high school, I started a job at Armco Steel and worked there until a close friend and I decided that we would join the army to avoid getting drafted and sent to Vietnam. We were under the false impression that the military was only sending people who had been drafted to the war zone and that if you volunteered for the "Buddy Plan," you could remain stateside. After basic training at Fort Benning, Georgia, we quickly found out that was not true. Our initial understanding was that when you enlisted with a friend, you would stay together no matter where you were assigned; however, as soon as basic training ended, I was sent to Fort Carson, Colorado, and my friend was sent to Fort Knox, Kentucky. It turned out that during Basic, we were alphabetically assigned to separate companies, so we did not see each other for the entire training period. Anyway, in less than a year, I found myself on the way to Vietnam. I had previously been apprised that my first cousin, who had gone before me, had been sent home after being severely wounded with shrapnel from an explosion in the field. That did not make it any easier on the mind. That may have been enough for my grandmother to insist that I attend church with her before leaving so the pastor could lay hands on me and pray for a safe return. I went and the pastor prayed and said the Lord told him that I would go and come back early and not have a single scratch on my body. As it turned out, my assigned duty station was with the 1st Infantry Division (also known as the Bloody Red One) in a city called Lai Khe, which was also nicknamed "Rocket City" because it received constant bombing from the enemy. I went, and my tour lasted ten months instead of a year, and when I returned home, it was indeed without a scratch. The time I spent there was as a mechanic/generator engineer stationed in the jungle in what was known as NDP Zones (Night Defensive Position).

I served in two of them. They were located away from base camps, and each was about the size of a football field but circular instead of rectangular. Constant gunfire and explosions were going on around us daily, and it was very nerve-racking. So much that I forgot about the promise that God would bring me home without a scratch. Before going to Vietnam, I never drank or smoked and was ignorant about participating in something that I knew was wrong. However, being in Vietnam changed my way of thinking. Fitting in with my fellow troops seemed extremely important at the time. I joined with several fellow soldiers and began to smoke pot and drink to calm my nerves. It worked, but I was so relaxed that I did not even think about the risk I was exposing myself to. Even though I came home scratch-free, I never thought about it until God reminded me years later. Despite the ignorance I subjected myself to, God kept me. My grandmother used to say that God takes care of children and fools. Hmm; I was not a child at the time.

Accepting Jesus means that God, full of grace and mercy, has received you into His glorious family. It is His wish that none shall perish. "And after you have suffered a little while, *the God of all grace, who has called you to his eternal glory in Christ, will restore, confirm, strengthen, and establish you."* (1 Peter 5:10). Restore the joy of your salvation and uphold me with a willing spirit. The Lord is my shepherd; I shall not want. God wants what is best for us, but unless we learn to establish His word in our lives, it will be challenging to reap the benefit of His benevolence. 2 Corinthians 5:17 teaches us that if anyone is in Christ, he is a new creation. The old has passed away; behold, the new has come. We can be assured that He has a plan for our lives through God's word. He clarifies that in Jeremiah 29:11 when He says, *"For I know the plans I have for you."* The Lord's declaration in His plan for us is for our welfare and not evil. Plans to give us a future and hope.

As previously mentioned, the word of God is a living word. It should be sown into our hearts, making it easier to propel our faith. We should always know that faith is an action word. It is a living and breathing "word" that will bring a positive harvest into our lives if we stand on it. The scriptures had been sown into my life at an early age that kept me even though I was so far off track. The Word says that all we need to have is faith the size of a mustard seed to receive God's blessings. I am thankful that I at least had that and was subconsciously aware that God never left me.

The promises of God are confirmed and available to all that are willing to receive the benefits it provides. If you have accepted Jesus as your Lord and Savior, and you are not reaping the help I am speaking of, I would encourage you to get before the Lord, pray and ask for direction. God will answer.

Scripture assures us of the following: *"God is not a man, that he should lie; neither the son of man, should repent: Hath he said, and shall he not do it? Or hath he spoken, and shall he not make it good?"* Numbers 23:19 KJV

In Matthew 11:28-30, Jesus says all those that labor and are heavily laden should come to Him, and He will give us rest. He assures us that if we take His yoke upon us and learn of Him, He will give us rest from our burdens.

The Book of Titus, Chapter 1, verse two states: "In the hope of eternal life, *which God; that cannot lie; promised before the world began.*" Although all things are possible with God, *three things are impossible* with Him: He cannot *lie, die*, and He cannot *fail.* We are to trust in the Lord with our hearts and lean not unto our understanding. When we acknowledge Him in all our ways, He will direct our paths. This is just one of the many promises of God. The more we learn, the stronger we become in Him. Consider a part of the recipe: God commands us to get wisdom and in all our getting to get understanding. In the same manner, Jesus instructs us that Man shall *not* live by bread *alone* but by every word that proceeded out of the mouth *of God.* We are taught that God orders the footsteps of the righteous. Following those footsteps can only bring more of God's favor into our lives.

After returning from Vietnam, I was stationed at Fort Leonard Wood, Missouri. I had a little over a year left to do in the army, so I decided to get married to my waiting fiancé. I could not wait to start a family and was comfortable that I was home safe and would no longer have to leave the country. It did not take long until she was pregnant with our first child. Unfortunately, the army had different plans. According to the military, at that time, if you had less than six months of duty left, being sent overseas was not supposed to happen. For me, it did not work that way. With six months and one day remaining, I was shipped to Germany and forced to leave my pregnant wife behind. By the time I returned, my daughter was six months old. I could not have been happier meeting her for the first time. I remember getting off the Greyhound bus, seeing her stretch her little arms for the first time, reaching for her daddy. Eager to get on with my life and no longer live under military constraints, I bought a home and finally settled in with my family. That was in 1971. I spent the next couple of years adjusting to what I thought was everyday life. I reunited with old friends and started to do things that I had learned to do in the service to fit in and be what I thought was a regular part of society. I went to work, drank, and smoked cigarettes and pot. It was vital for me to be accepted and considered "cool." Just down the street from where I always seemed to get involved in questionable conduct while trying to fit in, was the church where my grandmother had attended (unfortunately, she passed away in December of 1971), about a year after my daughter was born. It seemed like no matter what condition I was in, every time I was in the vicinity of that church, something inside would pull at me. Sometimes I would wonder if it was not the left-over influence of my grandmother's prayers for my wellbeing.

As time went on, my wife became pregnant again, and in February of 1974, we had a son. Realizing that I needed to grasp life better, I applied for an apprenticeship program at Armco and was accepted. The program was good, and I thought it would change my perception of life, but it did not. I kept going down the same old road. However, I believe God had a different plan for me. I was on my way to see some friends one night and was stopped by a Highway Patrolman. Instead of writing me a speeding ticket, he offered me the opportunity to apply for an Ohio State Highway Patrol position. This was when there were very few Black people on the force. I took advantage of the opportunity and initially failed the interview because I had admitted to using pot in the past. It had been over a year since I had smoked pot, so I started to feel like all the odds were against me and that change would not happen in my life. I had taken a two-hour trip to Columbus, Ohio for this interview and was sure I would be accepted. I was turned down on a Wednesday and was about to leave the office when they asked if I would be willing to reapply in a year. I gave an enthusiastic response of yes and left. On the way home, I was still able to lock into hope. On that Friday, I received a call asking if I was still interested. I said yes and was told if I could be there by Monday at 6:00 am, I could start the academy. The change had finally arrived, and I walked away from my old life feeling confident about a "new beginning."

Chapter 6

CHANGE YOUR WAYS- CHANGE YOUR DAYS

Upon understanding the power and authority we have in Christ, we should never be overcome or defeated by life's challenges. Difficult times will enter our lives, but we will always have victory as we live in Christ. Proverbs 3:5-6 says, *"Trust in the Lord with all your heart, and lean not unto your own understanding; In all your ways acknowledge Him, And He shall direct your paths."* This scripture should be committed to memory as part of the foundation for changing our ways of thinking about life. We have established what makes us righteous in Chapter 5. Bearing that in mind, we can apply that knowledge to the following: *"Even the righteousness of God which is by faith of Jesus Christ unto all and upon all them that believe: for there is no difference:"* Romans 3:22. It is a scripture that reminds us of God's faithfulness, and it encourages us to trust Him and furthermore, that He is worthy of our trust.

From the moment we are born, we enter into a life of sin that will require continuous change. Life is a constant evolutionary process, and change is an ongoing part. Nothing nor anyone stays the same. This is especially true when we become born again. Our new birth, after being spiritually awakened, will bring an enormous amount of change to our lives daily. 2 Corinthians 5:17 assures us, *"Therefore if any man is in Christ, he is a new creature: old things are passed away; behold, all things become new."* As a result, we change by walking or turning away from specific activities that were part of our former lives, and to be renewed in the spirit of our minds. In this way we put on the new self, created after the likeness of God in true righteousness and holiness.

The Bible says, so as a man thinketh, so is he. Each of us lives in our world of thought, and we can change every condition, good or bad, that enters our lives. Working patiently and intelligently on our thoughts and thought processes, we can and should remake our lives and transform our situations and circumstances to create a more beneficial and holy style of living. In Jeremiah 29:11, God says, *"For I know the thoughts that I think toward you, saith the LORD, thoughts of peace, and not of evil, to give you an expected end."* This promise of God can only be received if we live our lives "on purpose" through our faith in our Lord and Savior. God has provided, and all we need to do is exercise our faith through our works to receive His blessings.

Having a family serves as a testament to how God feels about His love for us. The good in us wants the absolute best things in life for our children, parents, brothers, sisters, and other relatives. Considering how strongly we feel about them, we can multiply those feelings regarding how God feels about us. His love spans as far as the east is from the west, making it indestructible and everlasting. He wants us to be holy because He is holy. This requires change, and every change in God's direction means favor because the closer we get to Him, the further we get from sin, and the cleaner our lives will be. At the end of the journey comes complete purification.

I reported for training at the Ohio State Highway Patrol Academy in October 1974. The training program was sixteen weeks of hard work. Sometimes, it was so difficult that cadets would sneak out at night and not return. The class started with approximately 130 candidates. Only thirty-eight of us graduated. Being one of the thirty-eight gave me a feeling of great accomplishment. It made me feel like I could conquer the world. At that time, there was a total of 1266 uniformed officers employed in the entire state, and it was my understanding that less than 50 of us were Black. That made it even more special because the racial aspect during those years was so out of balance, and I felt like I was making a difference.

After graduating in February of the following year, I was assigned to the Georgetown Highway Patrol Post in Brown County, Ohio. Unexpectedly, I found myself in an interracially biased position. There was no problem at the post or with my fellow officers; they all seemed very welcoming and respectful. The problem was more with the residents of the County. It quickly became evident that the threat of being subjected to the authority of a Black Highway Patrol Officer did not sit well with a predominantly white society. After being assigned to a coach, the journey began. During my patrols, the CB radio system was flooded with extreme racial slurs referring to me as the Chocolate Smokey, the Chocolate Drop, and the "N-word." Everyone heard the chatter, but no one spoke of it for several years.

As I look back on those times, I can tell you I would not be here if not for God's intervention. Although I believed in God, I was not fully living the lifestyle that would come close to representing Him. But that was getting much closer to changing. While under the direction of a senior officer coaching me, and within the first 90 days of my new post-assignment, we received a call to watch out for two prison escapees. It was not even ten minutes after receiving the call that we saw them. I was driving, so I turned to pursue the vehicle they had stolen. During the pursuit, gunshots were exchanged, and my coach received a minor gunshot wound to one of his hands. As he moved his hand around from the pain, blood splattered everywhere. Within seconds another bullet came through the windshield, missing my head by about six inches. At my coach's insistence, I continued in pursuit until the prisoners crashed their vehicle. As it turned out, there were five of them, not just two. They were all arrested but one, who about six months later was apprehended and taken into custody in Florida after running a traffic signal. After capturing those four, my coach and I returned to the patrol post and completed the paperwork. I felt intense but confident and firm. I didn't think about it at the time, but it had to be God who gave me the courage and the strength to continue as I did. And I believe it was He who stopped that bullet from going through my head and preserved my life in that dangerous situation.

After going home to my wife and family, the realization of what I had just gone through took its toll. As the tension left my body, I found myself shaking like a leaf hanging from a tree on a windy day. That realization and sense of protection that God provided enabled me to continue with a new level of confidence in my work.

On another occasion, after completing my probationary period, a lady I stopped for speeding insisted that I provide her with a form of identification other than the patrol vehicle I was driving and the uniform I was wearing. When I refused and insisted that she give me her driver's license and registration, she practically threw them at me. It was a windy day in April, so I was tempted to let the wind take them down the road and write her a citation for not having either of them; but I didn't. However, I did write the citation for speeding. This episode was a prime example of the interactions that would follow. All the while I hoped for a change in people's attitudes regarding an authority figure like myself being Black.

Another time, I clocked a vehicle driving over seventy miles per hour on a two-lane highway in a fifty-five mile per hour zone. I wrote the driver a citation and sent him on his way. The very next day, his father began harassing me daily. As soon as he knew I was on the road, he would start to sling racial slurs left and right. Although we knew that it was him, I was told there was nothing that could be done about it. It was the kind of harassment I was forced to ignore for years to come.

The antagonistic attitudes did not stop with whites; Black people, who I thought would be respectfully happy about us breaking the color barrier, were also critical of my achievement and considered me an "Uncle Tom" and a race trader. What's funny about the whole thing (if any humor could be recognized) was that the only place that I felt comfortable was among an all-white patrol post of state troopers who did not seem to see color. A few years passed, and I was happy that finally another Black State Trooper was assigned to our patrol post.

I worked in Brown County for close to seven years as the harassment continued on a regular basis. I thanked God that inside the Ohio State Highway Patrol structure was the kind of unity that made me feel like I was not alone. I later transferred to the next county of Clermont, but not before enduring a personal family tragedy. It turned out to be the start of another new beginning in my life. I will speak more on that in a separate section called "The Story of D.J." (Donita JoAnn Sanders)

Chapter 7

TRIALS AND TRIBULATIONS

Every promise of God is guaranteed because of His favor. Given that I have received so much of that, I would like to take this opportunity to share. Even when we don't see it right away, His blessings surround us every second of our lives. Giving the next breath is an act of favor that many of us don't think about or consider. We go through life receiving the gift of a breath, having a heartbeat, and the ability to think and have movement, but most of us don't give these things a second thought because they are a standard expectation of everyday life. We should always be thankful that God is full of mercy and grace and willing to provide favor for our benefit.

The Story of DJ

Donita Joann Sanders (D. J.)

Before leaving Brown County, I had a typical day on patrol when I received an emergency call to report to Children's Hospital in Cincinnati. My 9-year-old daughter, D. J. had just had a seizure and had been rushed to emergency. It took thirty days for the doctors to diagnose the cause. Finally, we were told that she was suffering from a rare disease called facial hemiatrophy.

The condition caused the side of her brain controlling her motor skills to stop working. At that time, the hope of finding a cure seemed next to impossible. Everyday life was obviously out of the question; as a matter of fact, trying to have any kind of life under these conditions seemed impossible. Our marriage soon began to fall apart because of the stress.

During my daughter's illness, my wife and I had been going to and from the hospital daily due to the seriousness of the situation. I continued working but did so on the evening shift so I could spend the days at the hospital. One evening, after being at the hospital all day, I accepted an extra shift (graveyard). While driving home that morning, I fell asleep and side-swiped a school bus. The driver said that it looked like I was sound asleep when he saw me coming straight at him. He told the investigating officer that he thought we would surely have a head-on collision. We were on a two-lane highway, and because of an embankment on the side of the road, the bus had nowhere to go. Suddenly, my car moved back into the right lane, but not before side-swiping the bus. We would have hit head-on had that not happened, and I could have been killed. It was more likely that I had been asleep for over twelve miles of winding road before reaching the bus because I didn't remember anything until after striking that bus. It's only by the grace of God that I survived.

Because of the stress levels, my wife and I decided to see a psychologist. I felt as if my wife was blaming the reason for our daughter's illness all on me. Instead of offering any suggestions for healing our emotional suffering, the psychologist advised my wife if she didn't feel she could handle things, that maybe she should move out. That was the last thing I expected to hear. Even though she suggested it, I never thought it would happen. A few weeks later, I came home from work one day and found my wife had taken all the furniture from our home and moved into Cincinnati. I was devastated.

I did not share this information with our daughter because I felt her medical situation was so delicate that the trauma would cause more problems. However, my wife felt differently about the case because the next time I saw D.J., she asked if she was the reason her mom and I were not together anymore. I told her, "No," while my heart melted from her asking.

One day while lying in bed and thinking about how frustrating life had become and trying to figure out why God had abandoned me, I became angry and shouted out; God, if you are so real, make the clock stop. I was referring to a radio clock on the nightstand next to my bed. As soon as the words cleared my mouth, the radio clock stopped playing, and I immediately became so fearful that I almost wet myself. After a moment or so, the clock started playing again. I began to rationalize that someone had probably had an accident and struck one of the electric poles in the area, or maybe we had experienced a power outage. When I went to work that afternoon, I checked the daily logs to find that not a single event had occurred that day. I never spoke to God that way again, and I started trying to get closer to Him, knowing that He was hearing everything I was saying.

After D.J. had been in the hospital for at least two years, I remember stopping a car for speeding. I asked the driver for his license and registration. When he gave it to me, I noticed that in his driver's license photo, he was wearing a collar around his neck like a priest. I asked where he was headed, and he said that he was going to a funeral somewhere in Kentucky. After giving back his license and registration, I told him to slow down and said he could go. At that moment, he said God had spoken and said to him that I was concerned about a loved one. He asked for my address and said he would like to stop and visit on his way back through. As a State Trooper, you never just give your address to a stranger. However, before I could think, I opened my mouth and blurted out the information. It was as if I had no control over my mouth. This occurred on a Friday morning, and I was off the next day. As I waited to hear from him, a part of me kept thinking that he was just being nice and friendly to get out of a ticket. But then, how would he know about my situation? When he finally showed up, we discussed D.J.'s illness. He told me to trust God, and everything would be all right. My hope was renewed, but DJ was still extremely sick, and I desperately hung on to my faith.

Sometime later, I attended an evening church service somewhere near the Cincinnati Zoo. I can't even remember the church's name or why I went. However, I remember the service as clear as a bell. The church was packed with a thousand people or more. It was so full that I had to sit on one of the rows closest to the rear. There were about five sections to the church and thirty rows deep. At the end of the praise and worship session, the pastor announced that there was a guest speaker. When the speaker took the stage, he said that God had given him the gift of speaking into people's lives. When God had a message for someone, He would show the speaker a light above the person's head so the message could be delivered and would direct him to that person.

I watched him go to several people and speak the Lord's word to them. While he was doing so, I remember thinking that God didn't have anything for me. As soon as those thoughts cleared, he started heading in my direction. I assumed he was looking at everyone but me. When he reached the row where I was sitting, he pointed directly at me and said, God wants you to know that the one you love and have been praying for will be coming home soon. As I tried to believe it, I felt even more aware of D.J.'s condition. I went home and waited impatiently. A week went by, and nothing. Another week went by, and still nothing. My faith weakened. Then, in the third week after the church service, I received a call informing me that I could pick up my daughter and bring her home.

Even though I could bring my daughter home, she still suffered from facial hemiatrophy. The disease had taken quite a toll on her body and her mind. Her face was severely disfigured on the right side, and she walked with a terrible limp. Her little body had been damaged to the point where she even had to use a walker to get around. Although she could understand what I was saying, it was challenging for her to talk. The disease affected the electrodes in her brain, so she could not correctly use her motor skills. It was a bittersweet period as I spent time with her, but she was back in the hospital in less than ten days because her condition continued to worsen. It wasn't long after that that she was transferred to a rest home near Warren County, Ohio. At that point, I felt like the hospital had given up on any chances of recovery. She was in the rest home for two years before she finally went into a coma. Her condition deteriorated to what doctors described as a vegetative state, and her only way of breathing was through the life support machine. At that point, we were asked to make the most difficult decision ever. We had to decide whether to keep her in a state of vegetation or to discontinue support and release her to God. We chose to let her go.

It had been a five-year journey whereby we had exhausted our $1,000,000 health insurance policy, gained $68,000 worth of additional expenses, and my family had been torn apart.

My question was: Where was God?

I don't know why God didn't heal my daughter. As much as I would like to, I don't have that answer. What I do know is this; He was there. He is always there. Earlier I spoke about an accident I was involved in with a school bus; He was there. He was there during the chase to capture prison escapees who fired a bullet missing my head by no more than six inches. During my daughter's illness, I held a gun to my head and wanted to pull the trigger so bad that my finger was twitching; He was there, also. He was there during the high-speed chases that I was involved in and driving over one hundred and twenty miles per hour.

I could go on and on with countless situations that could have ended my life; He was there.

Whether or not we can experience or sense God, *He is always there with us in our trouble*. His presence is an objective fact, even when we can't feel Him. This is why we pray, stay in the Word, and seek the Holy Spirit. I believe that I will see my daughter again, along with all of my other loved ones who accepted Jesus as Lord and Savior. I can feel it in my spirit, and that was even before I read any scripture in that regard. I am confident that God's promise to see D.J. and other loved ones lost was given to me by the Lord Himself because of the peace that came with the deliverance of His word.

1 Thessalonians 4:13-18 ESV *"But we do not want you to be uninformed, brothers, about those who are asleep, that you may not grieve as others do who have no hope. For since we believe that Jesus died and rose again, even so, through Jesus, God will bring with him those who have fallen asleep. For this, we declare to you by a word from the Lord that we who are alive, who are left until the coming of the Lord, will not precede those who have fallen asleep. For the Lord himself will descend from heaven with a cry of command, an archangel's voice, and the sound of God's trumpet. And the dead in Christ will rise first. Then we who are alive, who are left, will be caught up together with them in the clouds to meet the Lord in the air, and so we will always be with the Lord. Therefore encourage one another with these words."* **This particular scripture is God's assurance that upon leaving this earth, there is an afterlife known as eternity. We will either spend it in Heaven or Hell.**

For me, the fact is that because of my faith in God, I will see my daughter again. And this time, it will be for eternity. Proverbs 3, verses 5 and 6 tell me that I should trust in the Lord with all of my heart and lean not unto my own understanding. The scripture promises that if I acknowledge Him in all my ways, He will direct my path. My path is to Heaven.

Chapter 8

FIGHTING THE GOOD FIGHT OF FAITH

What does it mean?

Fighting the good fight of faith involves *running from sin and pursuing things such as righteousness, godliness, faith, love, endurance, and gentleness.* Fighting the good fight of faith is about following God's will and a life of faith, daily. God has given us "free will." We have the right to choose our direction in life and not be bound by those things that appeal to our fleshly nature. However, this requires focus and education in the things of God.

For example: If it's hard to turn away from harmful activities such as gambling, it would be because we have allowed the seeds of that particular sin to become embedded in our lives. We have been given the authority over all the power of the enemy, and Jesus says that nothing by any means shall cause us harm. Focusing on God's word enables us to dig those seeds up and move in the right direction. The reality is that everything has a beginning and an end. That means there is some form of control involved in creating, using, or discontinuing the involvement of sin in our lives.

It all starts with change. We must use prayer, faith, and acceptance of the Word of God. As previously stated, one of the things that God absolutely cannot do is lie. Therefore, when He says we have the power, we do. That means the decisions boil down to a matter of choice. This is where "free will" comes in. It is yours to do what you will. Just saying it sounds easy; however, it's not.

I remember reading in the Book of Job where the sons of God (the angels) came together, and Satan was among them. After God asked where he had been, he answered that he had been going to and fro in the earth and walking up and down in it. God asked if he had considered His servant Job and this was the beginning of the devil's attack against Job. Just like Job, we are subject to the attacks of Satan. Later, in the New Testament, in 1st Peter we are warned to be sober and vigilant because our enemy, the devil, walks about like a roaring lion looking for anyone he can devour. That would essentially be anyone who is not already under his control or anyone attempting to escape from under his influence. We must never make the mistake of thinking he doesn't exist or that he isn't looking to take advantage of us. He is our enemy and would like nothing more than to make us think that he doesn't exist so that his work will be more effective.

It is crucial to realize that we wake up to a war every day. It's a war that began the day we were born and will continue until the day we die. It's not a war fought with guns and other physical weapons; this war is much more deadly, and the most valuable thing at stake is our souls. John 10:10 tells us this: The thief (which is Satan) does not come except to steal, kill, and destroy. Jesus says: "I have come that they may have life and have it more abundantly."

One of the Devil's most potent weapons is fear. Think about times that you've done the opposite of what you should have because you were afraid what the results might be; and then afterward, you found your initial direction would have been the right way to go. I'm sure you can think of many situations that are like this. By its very nature, fear causes division and rips us apart, and instills doubt about the goodness of God. Instead of relying on our faith to pull us through, it's what causes us to give in and quit when things aren't going our way. It's also important to understand that fear is not always accompanied with shaking and trembling. Sometimes it can present itself in the form of over-confidence adorned by extreme caution. It's that sense of pride that comes before a fall. We have to learn to wait on God with a level of faith that tells us that no matter what, God is in control, and the outcome of our situations is in His hands and will be in our best interest. Sometimes, even if it's not what we thought we should have, we must trust God that He has our best interest at heart. I know I said it before, but I'll repeat it because it's so important. If we trust in the Lord with all of our hearts and view things from God's perspective, He will direct our paths, and it will be a path of righteousness.

Another of the Devil's potent weapons is deception. Playing with our minds causes us to see things differently than the way they are. The use of deception doesn't always have to involve lying. Sometimes it's twisting the truth or presenting true things misleadingly or deceptively.

Deception can also be an act or form of misrepresentation; that makes people feel or begin to feel betrayed while sewing distrust between those having challenging relationships.

It's a practice that disregards God's law of sowing and reaping. We tend to hurt ourselves and those we love and care for the most. It's always wise to test every spirit with the Word of God. The truth will always set you free.

As we enter into battle, we must remind ourselves that God is not man that He should lie. His word is truth, and His promises are infallible. Hebrews 10 says that we are to "Hold fast the profession of our faith without wavering; for He is faithful that promised." We are to know God and learn to trust His word. As we move forward, I will share some of the most potent and compelling scriptures from God's word that I've heard in my lifetime.

The first scripture I find most compelling is Isaiah 54:17 KJV: *"No weapon formed against thee shall prosper, and every tongue that shall rise against thee in judgment thou shalt condemn. This is the heritage of the servants of the LORD, and their righteousness is of me, saith the LORD."*

In the beginning, I had a tough time accepting the weight of this scripture. It didn't make sense as things in my life always seemed to be working against me, given that many of the problems I endured were my fault. Of course, there's no way I thought it would be me at that time because it was so much easier to pass the blame elsewhere. As I began to study God's word, I discovered that it was easier to receive what He was telling me when I started to focus on what I was learning. For example, let's take the verse, *"No weapon formed against me shall prosper."* It didn't mean that no weapon would ever form, but that *they would not prosper.* Sometimes, the negative things in our lives require us to hunker down in our faith (fighting the good fight of faith) and not give in to defeat.

We are to hold fast and trust in God while using His word to bring us victory. God never gives us more than we can manage; fighting through those tough times can aid in increasing our faith and make us much more potent.

Another part of this scripture that was confusing for me was the part about every tongue that shall rise against thee in judgment, thou shall condemn. So, I kept waiting for Him to condemn those that wrongfully accused me. I later realized that the word "thou" referred to me and that exercising my faith using the word of God would bind the tongues of my enemies. I had to get it sown into my spirit that God's word is undeniably sound. He says He will never leave, forsake, or fail me. If I rightfully depend on His word, and His word doesn't work, that makes Him a liar; that is something God cannot and will not ever be. As I make specific references to the scriptures, remember that God is no respecter of persons, meaning that what He will do for one, He'll do for others. Once we have accepted His Son, Jesus, as Lord and Savior, the Blood of Jesus covers us completely. As we move through life, our victories are imminent. Life is going to happen. It's how we deal with it that makes the difference. I was talking to a close friend of mine one time, and something she said hit like a ton of bricks and had so much meaning that I've never forgotten it and think of it often. She said this:

"If you haven't had a head-on collision with the devil lately, you may want to check yourself to ensure you're not going in the same direction as He is. Once again, it's a reminder of The First Epistle of Peter (5:8) tells us to "*be sober and vigilant; because your adversary, the devil, as a roaring lion, walketh about, seeking whom he may devour.*" His entire purpose is to kill, steal, and destroy through lies and deception.

Another of my favorite and most meaningful scriptures is Luke 10:19-20. Jesus said: *"Behold, I give unto you power to tread on serpents and scorpions, and over all of the power of the enemy: and nothing shall by any means hurt you. Notwithstanding in this rejoice not that the spirits are subject unto you; but rather rejoice, because your names are written in heaven."*

There are two indisputable guarantees in these scripture verses. One is that when using His word, we are assured of victory, and two, our names are written in Heaven. It's like having a reservation in Eternity.

These are just some of the greatest weapons of warfare that God has provided for our protection. We benefit entirely when we come to know and understand them. I have to remind myself of their power often, and I encourage you to do the same. Knowing our faith's power helps us use these weapons more effectively. This is why God tells us to get wisdom, and in all of our getting, to gain understanding. It's proven, time after time, that knowledge is a great and powerful thing when shared with the right intent and purpose. Although knowledge is a tool, it can also be a weapon. When knowledge is shared without regard for the ramifications of its release, it can be more damaging than any storm, more shattering than any blow. Knowledge used appropriately has the power to make significant changes not only in our lives but also in the lives of others.

Another immensely powerful scripture that provides protection and wisdom for success and survival is Ephesians 6:10-15 NIV; *"Finally, be strong in the Lord and his mighty power. Put on the whole armor of God so that you can take your stand against the devil's schemes. For our struggle is not against flesh and blood, but against the rulers, against the authorities, against the powers of this dark world, and the spiritual forces of evil in the heavenly realms. Therefore, put on the whole armor of God, so that when the day of evil comes, you may be able to stand your ground, and after you have done everything, to stand. Stand firm then, with the belt of truth buckled around your waist, with the breastplate of righteousness in place, and with your feet fitted with the readiness from the gospel of peace.*

Putting on the whole armor of God:

To put on the whole armor of God is to apply all of the Gospel to all of your life. The entire armor expresses *your trust in God and what He has done for you through Jesus Christ.* Your victory in spiritual warfare was secured at the cross of Christ and the blood that was shed there. Revelations 12:11 states the following: *"And they overcame him by the blood of the Lamb, and by the word of their testimony, and they loved not their lives unto the death. Therefore, rejoice ye heavens and ye that dwell in them."*

There are seven pieces to the Armor of God:

1. **Belt of Truth -** The belt of truth prevents us from falling prey to the devil's lies. We must have a solid understanding of the truth, or the rest of the armor is useless. If we wear it crooked or have no belt, we'll have difficulty gripping the Sword of the Spirit (God's word) in time and risk exposing our more vital organs. We must know the truth and be able to deliver His word without hesitancy.

2. **The Breastplate of Righteousness** - Being righteous means being correct, especially morally. Do right because it is accurate. Just as we put off wrongdoing in changing our lives to become more like God, we are to stay on that path of righteousness,

reaching out to become more holy in our actions because God is holy.

3. **The Sword of the Spirit** - This is the word of God. Arm yourself daily with scripture. We should fill our hearts on a constant and continual basis, so when the need arises, the living word of God will automatically come to mind. Occasionally, I have engaged in conversations where the word spews from inside as it automatically speaks on my behalf. It reassures me that I am fully armed.

4. **Shield of Faith -** God is our shield. He cares about us as individuals and is invested in our well-being. He wants us to put our hope in Him, even when everything around us is screaming that it would be foolish to do so; God has us covered from head to toe, inside and out. We are to place our complete trust in Him; every minute, every second, and every hour of the day.

5. **Shod our feet in the Gospel of Peace** - Having our feet fitted with the shoes of the gospel of peace *allows us to be ready to share God with others.* As Christians, we should always be prepared, as we never know when an opportunity may arise to share the gospel's good news with someone.

6. **Helmet of Salvation** - Keeping your mind filled with the word of God and knowing that God's word i*s* quick, powerful, and sharper than any two-edged sword; piercing soul, and spirit, and is a discerner of the thoughts and intents of the heart so as not to allow deception to penetrate your being.

7. **Gird our Loins** – Be prepared to take on challenging tasks if and when necessary. This means to be ready mentally, physically, or both.

The Armor of God is necessary for survival through this war between spirits and principalities and should not be taken lightly. Your sincere efforts will be recognized by God the Father and blessed with His favor because of the work of faith you demonstrate.

No one can escape sin. Every day of our lives, we are either involved in or confronted by it. In the Christian environment, we often hear that we are engaged in spiritual warfare; a part of that warfare is how we handle sin. If we are not sinning, we are at least exposed to it somehow. It might only be as a witness—hearing or seeing sinful acts. The challenge for us is to be strong enough in the power of God's might, recognize it for what it is, and use God's word appropriately for our protection. Thus, we must work through faith.

Chapter 9

THE FAVOR OF GOD AGAINST ALL ODDS

Ephesians 2:8-9

> *"For by grace are ye saved through faith; and that not of yourselves: it is the gift of God: Not of works, lest any man should boast."*

Once we accept Jesus as our Lord and Savior, there is absolutely nothing else we can do to earn God's favor. This is because we already have it. It is a gift that God gives. No man can say he deserved it or received it because of his works.

I have realized that faith requires unyielding focus. There's an old saying that suggests that what you don't use, you lose. The concept of that saying is genuine from several perspectives. First of all, from my point of view, it's important to be like a sponge. A sponge that does not hold water becomes dry and eventually brittle. It starts to crack and ultimately falls apart, becoming useless. If you continually soak that sponge in water, it remains soft, flexible, and clean. If we allow our bodies to work like sponges and use the Word of God as the water, we stay full, we are always cleansed.

It was during my daughter's illness that my wife and I divorced. I was granted custody of our son, and my wife received custody of our daughter. I transferred my job to the next county, hoping for a fresh start. I had left the Highway Patrol, feeling the need for something more.

One of my younger brothers had been living in California and I let him convince me that moving there was exactly the fresh start I needed. While sharing my intentions with one of my best friends, she said that she also wanted to move to California, so I invited her to come along.

Since my car had gotten repossessed because of the extreme debt I had accumulated during my daughter's illness, my initial intention was to fly out and stay with my brother until I could get back on my feet. But my friend Kristi, who decided to join me, had a car which changed everything. We packed up her Volkswagen full of all our possessions and with $1238 between us to cover our expenses, we hit the road.

Kristi had an old English Standard Bible that her mother had left her, so we put it on the dashboard and agreed that God would be our guide. Instead of going to San Diego, where my brother lived, I accepted an interview in Irwindale, California. I got the job as an aassistant project manager for a security company working at Miller Brewing Company, so we lived out of a hotel in San Dimas. It might be hard to see how landing a job at a brewery would be walking in the footsteps of the righteous, but sometimes you have to walk through the wilderness to get to where God wants you to be.

After I started to work, Kristi and I shared her car. Eventually, one of my co-workers decided to sell me one of his cars, so I could finally have my own transportation.

Once I got the car, Kristi moved into a condo with a girlfriend she had met at work. Although things seemed to be going well, the girlfriend's parents decided to sell the condominium. As a result, Kristi and I agreed that she should move back in with me. I had gotten an apartment for myself, and things had started going well. After about a year and a half, Kristi and I developed a relationship, and by grace, we married. I felt restoration in my life, and my focus began to change.

The more I focused, the better life became. I knew I had to change direction, and I did.

Something inside of me felt renewed and my life was moving in a different direction. I could see a future and started to set new goals for myself. At work, I focused on and received promotions. With Kristi I had a newfound love, and life became more exciting as we became more involved in different ministries helping others through some of the same challenges we had faced. We were blessed and God's favor didn't stop there. He blessed us with a daughter, and we decided that our life would be about the three of us, and of course, God. We vowed that we would live our lives for each other and that no one or nothing would ever come between us.

At the writing of this book, we have been together for thirty-five years and counting. The closer we got to God, the more blessed our lives became. Did we have challenges? Yes. God's heritage to us is this: No weapon formed against us shall prosper, and we shall condemn every tongue that shall rise against us in judgment. Our understanding of this has been a blessing because we know that God doesn't lie. As a result, we realize that God didn't say that weapons won't form; but He did say they will not prosper. That has been so evident in our lives that I have to reflect on some of those instances:

1. I remember when we were so broke that we couldn't afford diapers, baby food, or even gas money for me to drive to work. I had to ride a bicycle 26 miles to and from work each way. I remember kneeling with Kris and praying to God and asking Him to make a way and provide. We felt devastated. As I was riding to work one day, I ran into money floating in the air. I grabbed three bills and stuffed them in my pocket without even leaving my bike. When I got to work, I checked to find I had forty-five dollars. I couldn't have been more excited. It never crossed my mind that God had answered our prayer. I only thought of it as an incredible stroke of luck. I called Kris and

gave her the good news. We were ecstatic with relief. I was in church about a year later when my mind zoned out during service, and I relived the entire event. In the process, I heard everything the Pastor was preaching. That's when I realized that the provision was from God. I felt happy for the blessing but guilty for not giving God the glory.

2. Kris and I were driving home from work on another occasion. At that time, we were both working in Pasadena and carpooled to and from work. On the way home one evening, a car driving about 65 mph, ran a stoplight and crashed into the side of our car. It hit us on the driver's side, causing us to spin into a three-hundred-and-sixty-degree circle. It was a hard enough strike to force the airbags to deploy on both sides of our car. We received enough damage that the car was unrepairable and had to be salvaged. The officer strongly encouraged us to go to the hospital and get checked out, but neither of us were hurt; we didn't even have a scratch. We were seen at the hospital and the doctor released us to go home after about a four-hour wait. Before impact, everything seemed to go into slow motion, and I remember seeing the driver, who looked more demonic than human. As an experienced accident investigator, after looking at the crash, it seemed impossible that we were able to walk away with no injuries at all. Seconds before the impact occurred, Kris said she felt God was telling her to fasten her seat belt. Almost as soon as God told her is when the crash happened. The only reasonable explanation is that God, once again, changed the odds in our favor.

3. There was a time when I was diagnosed with an enlarged heart. The doctors said that test results showed one side of my heart was twice the size of the other half. During a visit to another church, the pastor announced that God told him that there were

people in the audience with complex medical challenges. He asked that they come to the front of the church so he could lay hands on them for healing. Several people went up, but I stayed in my seat. Instead of continuing, the pastor said, "someone didn't come." Kris started elbowing me in the side, telling me to get up there. I did so reluctantly. The pastor began to speak, and when it came time for me, he laid hands and prayed for God to heal my body. I didn't feel a thing and went back to my seat to enjoy the rest of the service. That week I had a second doctor's appointment to see a specialist. After the examination, he looked at me and said, "I'm not sure why they sent you to me; you have the heart of a 19-year-old." That was over twenty years ago, and I haven't had a problem with my heart since. To me, it was just more evidence that God is in control.

4. In Chapter 6, I talked about the bullet that missed my head by about six inches. Again, proof of the favor of God working against all odds.

5. One evening, I was washing dishes at the kitchen sink. Suddenly Kris started yelling about my bleeding from the nose. I had no clue what she was talking about until I looked down at the dishwater. It was turning blood red from my nosebleed. Kris drove me to the hospital emergency room as I pinched my nose to stop the bleeding. Upon our arrival, I was immediately taken to the back. After being treated, the doctor told me that my blood pressure was over 400, and he could not understand how I could even walk into the hospital. They kept me overnight for observation, and because my condition was so much better, I was released to go home. The weapon formed against me did not prosper because God stopped it in its tracks. Praise God.

6. One Sunday during service, there was an opportunity to give to one of the elderly women of the church. We were told that the person in need was always asking for handouts and that we shouldn't give because it only encourages her to continue. Kris and I were surprised at the response, but we both, without hesitation, decided to give her our last $80 we had to last us for the remainder of the week. After going home, we changed clothes and decided to run a few errands before settling in for the afternoon. As we backed out of the driveway, Kris said to stop the car. I did, and she got out and picked something up off the street. When she got back inside the car, I noticed she had a small wad of money which amounted to exactly $80. Scripture says that we are to "give, and it shall be given to us; good measure pressed down, shaken together, and running over, shall man give into your bosom". After giving our last $80, God immediately gave it back.

7. In 1997, we decided to buy a new home. After going through the most significant part of the buying process, we were told we had to come up with a little over $1300 for carpeting. We argued that carpeting should be included in the overall cost of the purchase. At that time, the builder didn't see it that way. So, we left the office trusting God to work on our behalf. We never know how God will bless us; we just need to have faith that He would. After praying, Kris and our daughter Teiler had to go to Vons grocery store. Upon entering the store, Teiler called out to Kris to look. There was a small pile of money lying in a group of watermelons. She picked it up and found the owner's name and a bank receipt. There was no other information. When they came home, we opened the phone book and found a number. When Kris contacted her, the lady was thrilled that we were honest enough to return her wallet with the $400 cash that was

with it. The lady shared that it happened to be the last of her money she had to bury her husband, who had recently passed.

The following weekend, we spoke with the realtor about any options available to secure the final purchase of our new home. The agent thought for a moment and said that she would like to pay the outstanding balance for us. We agreed and felt that once again, the favor of God overcame the odds on our behalf because we were honest in our actions and returned the money that was not ours because it was the right thing to do.

I could talk and list all the events where God has demonstrated His favor in our lives. We have been the victors, but only through Christ Jesus. Romans 8:37 says, "*Nay, we are more than conquerors through him that loved us in all these things.*" If we pray, hope, and trust in His Word, God's work will be evident in all of our lives. He is no respecter of persons, and what He does for one, He will do for others regardless of one's social status or prestige. We have to trust in the Lord with all of our hearts and allow Him to direct our paths. Once we accept Jesus as our Lord and Savior, we become righteous through His blood.

Chapter 10

WHAT MAKES US RIGHTEOUS?

It is critical to understand that there are two kinds of righteousness. There is the righteousness of man, and then there is the righteousness of God.

Let's start with the definition of righteous from the Merriam-Webster dictionary:

1: Act according to the divine or moral law: free from guilt or sin. 2a: morally right or justifiable, a righteous decision. b: arising from an outraged sense of justice or morality righteous indignation.

Moving forward, you will see that the definition of righteousness is recognized through a general concept by society. Righteousness is the quality of being virtuous, honorable, or morally right. It can also refer to expected social behavior. Righteousness is the noun form of the adjective, righteous. Being righteous means doing what is right and obeying the law or adhering to moral standards, whether legally established or not. Since we live in a world where people tend to believe that their ways are the best and suitable in their own eyes, it is hard for many people to accept the absolute standard of righteousness.

True or false becomes relative, and many believe they can do whatever they think, or feel is right. Here we will discover why the Bible's views on righteousness stands out among the different beliefs and values this world offers. The fact is that regardless of how righteous you are according to man, it doesn't fit you into the same category under the standards of God. For example, some think they will go to

Heaven because they are good persons and do good things. Nothing can be further from the truth. There is only one way to be truly righteous, and that is to be cleansed by the word of God.

It cannot be denied that righteousness is an attribute that belongs to God and is manifested in Him. Not one individual can be justified by his works apart from God's ordinance. Therefore, righteousness is a beautiful gift from God to humanity through His love: it is the God-given quality imputed to humankind upon believing in and accepting the Son of God as your Lord and Savior.

When we look at man's righteousness compared to the righteousness of God, the standards of humanity and the quality of being morally accurate and justifiable appear solely based on the adherence of behavior according to regulations, constitutions, or concepts established by man in the context of a nation.

When we consider a deeper, more spiritual meaning, righteousness is the quality of being right in the eyes of God. This includes:

- **character** (or nature which is the phenomena of the physical world, including plants, animals, the landscape, and other features and products of the earth, as opposed to humans or human creations.)

- **conscience** (or attitude, which is defined as a settled way of thinking or feeling about someone or something, typically one that is reflected in a person›s behavior.)

- **conduct** (actions that represent a person's behavior, especially on a particular occasion or context.)

- **command** (a single distinct meaningful element of speech or writing, used with others or sometimes alone to form a sentence and typically shown with a space on either side when written or printed.)

Therefore, righteousness is based on God's standard because He is the ultimate Law giver (Isaiah 33:22). The laws of nature, such as gravity, motion, energy conservation, etc., originated by the Creator and reveal that the God of the universe is the God of order (Psalm 33:5, 36:6). However, the laws of God do not only comprise the laws of nature. In the Bible, the laws of God are demonstrated in His righteousness, which regulates the God-human relationship as the foundation of the relationship between humans and their neighbors (Psalm 9:8).

Righteousness is a gift from God and cannot be earned or attained through any man's own efforts apart from God's ordinance. We, as humans, are inclined to follow our paths and use our ways instead of God's. (This selfish desire for independence from God is in our nature, we were born into it, and we need nobody to teach us that; however, we always need the discipline to remain faithful to walk with God). According to Isaiah 64:6, compared to the righteousness of God, our righteous deeds are "nothing but filthy rags." The good news is that it's not about our achievements or accomplishments.

Righteousness is a beautiful gift from God to humanity through Christ's act of love. We can easily see the righteousness of God as it is manifested consistently throughout the entire Bible.

The Righteousness of God stems back to the Old Testament. Since the fall of man, sin entered the world and caused wickedness in man's heart. Subsequently, the law is given due to the rebellious nature of humankind. Although righteousness is accounted for by those who carefully observe all God's commandments (Deuteronomy 6:25, 13:17-18), the law reveals that no man can satisfy all its requirements. It exposes our helplessness toward accomplishing God's perfect standard.

Merciful and gracefully, God has always rewarded humanity with His righteousness by faith, not by works (even since the Old Testament era). The word "righteousness" in the Bible first appears in the account of God's covenant with Abraham when he believed in the promise of his future offspring (Genesis 15:6); that was even before he was called

Abraham, a father of many nations (signifying that God's plan would never fail despite our past behaviors).

The way of righteousness leads to life, not death (Proverbs 12:28) because God is the ultimate source of all life. It means that "righteousness" belongs to God alone, and therefore as we pursue God, we find His holiness. Seeking God's righteousness means putting God at the center of our lives. And here is the truth: God takes pleasure in those who pursue justice (Proverbs 15:9, 21:3, 21:21).

The Righteousness of God in the New Testament

Since the death and resurrection of Christ, the purpose of the law has been fulfilled, and as a result, *"everyone who believes in Him is made right with God"* (Romans 3:22, 10:4). Christ is the perfect revelation of God. *"Thus, our faith in Him leads us to the righteousness of God"* (Romans 1:17). *"Believing in Christ is the work of faith, not the work of the flesh, which produces character"* (Romans 4:5-6). Stated another way, righteousness is the God-given quality gifted to man upon believing in Christ.

When Jesus died on the cross, He bore all sins of humanity and became sin for us. As a result, *"everyone who believes in Him is made righteous with God"* (2 Corinthians 5:21, 1 Peter 2:24).

The sacrifice of Jesus as the Son of God is the only thing that makes us righteous in the eyes of God. No other eyes matter. Accepting Jesus as our Lord and Savior requires us to work through the entire acceptance process. In other words: If we don't allow Him to be our Lord, it stands to reason that He can't possibly be our Savior. We can claim it all day with our mouths, but the words are meaningless unless they live in our hearts and flows from inside.

According to Matthew 15:19-20: *"For out of the heart proceed evil thoughts, murders, adulteries, fornications, thefts, false witness, blasphemies: These are the things that defile: but to eat with unwashed hands defile not a man."*

It has been said that an overwhelming feeling will express itself in speech; however, it should also be noted that Matthew 12:34 says: "*Out of the abundance of the heart the mouth speaketh.*"

We should all ask ourselves what God sees when He looks at our hearts?

Chapter 11

God Doesn't Require Perfection, Just Faith.

God does not require us to be perfect. He only requires faith. Following the word of God is a demonstration of how we exercise that faith. In the spiritual context, faith is a verb, and a verb is a word that conveys action. We should always be mindful that when we exercise our faith, we should be doing something that causes us to move toward doing and acquiring those desires. Scripture tells us that God wants to give us the desires of our hearts. Psalm 37:4 confirms just that; *"Take delight in the LORD, and he will provide you with* the *desires of your heart.*" Do what the LORD wants, and he will give you your heart's desire. Of course, this desire may be denied if the desire goes against God's word. He cannot and will not compromise His word. Throughout this book, you find God is a God of love, and nothing He makes stands for evil or the provision of evil desires.

Therefore, when we ask, ask with that in mind. Our request should mean what is good and decent.

In other words, do not ask amiss, which would be asking wrongly.

For example, any motivation in our sinful flesh will not be pleasing to God if it results from pride, anger, revenge, a sense of entitlement, or a desire for approval.

The title of this chapter is "God Doesn't Require Perfection, Just Faith." I want to expand on the title just a bit. God knows that we cannot accomplish perfection at any level on our own. However, if we are in Christ, we can do all things. I have to believe that achieving perfection is included. What I mean is that it's possible to achieve perfection at some level; but we, as humankind, will never be perfect. Therefore, our goals should reflect the character of God and not our own. In accepting Jesus as our Lord and Savior, we should realize that Jesus is the vine, and we are the branches. As we abide in Him, he will "abide" in us. In Him lies perfection, and in Him, we are protected, and our lives are fruitful because of it. This is established in the Book of John 15:5; and furthermore, that apart from Jesus, we can do nothing.

One of the reasons God doesn't expect perfection from us is because if we are in Him, we are in perfection, which causes us to be perfect in Christ Jesus. Again, apart from Him, we can do nothing, but in Him, we are perfected. What it boils down to is a matter of perfection vs. reality. Perfection is reality; however, we are far from it until we are in Christ. We were born into sin and are flawed.

Becoming a Christian (previously known as a follower of God) is not a call to perfection. If we were perfect, what part of our lives would require a need for God? We are to bring ourselves to God as a "living sacrifice."

Before we get into this, let's define what a living sacrifice is not. It is not trying to be perfect doing anything equal to the capability of Jesus. He is the ultimate sacrifice and the only reason we can communicate with God. He is the pathway to Heaven and is the Way, the Truth, and the Life: No one comes to the Father except through Jesus (John 14:6-7).

Now back to defining a "Living Sacrifice":

In Romans 12:1, Paul says, *"I beseech you therefore, brothers, by the mercies of God to present your bodies a living sacrifice, holy, pleasing to God, which is your reasonable service."* Paul's admonition to the believers in Rome was to sacrifice themselves to God, not as a sacrifice on the altar, as the Mosaic Law required the sacrifice of animals, but as a *living* sacrifice. The dictionary defines *sacrifice* as "anything consecrated and offered to God." As believers, how do we consecrate and offer ourselves to God as a living sacrifice?

Under the Old Covenant, God accepted the sacrifices of animals. But these were just a foreshadowing of the gift of the Lamb of God, Jesus Christ. Because of His ultimate, once-for-all-time sacrifice on the cross, the Old Testament sacrifices became obsolete and are no longer of any effect (Hebrews 9:11-12). The only acceptable worship for those in Christ is to offer ourselves entirely to the Lord. Under God's control, the believer's yet unredeemed body can and must be yielded to Him as an instrument of righteousness (Romans 6:12-13; 8:11-13). Because of the ultimate sacrifice of Jesus for us, this is only "reasonable."

What does a living sacrifice look like in the practical sense?

The following verse from Romans 12:2 helps us to understand. We are a living sacrifice for God by not being conformed to this world. The world is defined for us in 1 John 2:15-16 as the lust of the flesh, the eyes, and the pride of life. All that the world offers can be reduced to these three things. The passion of the flesh includes everything that appeals to our appetites and involves excessive desires for food, drink, sex, and anything else that satisfies physical needs. Lust of the eyes mainly involves materialism, coveting whatever we see that we don't have, and envying those who have what we want. The pride of life is defined by any ambition for that which puffs us up and puts us on the throne of our own lives.

How can believers *not* be conformed to the world? By being "transformed by the renewing of our minds." We do this primarily through the power of God's Word to transform us. We need to hear Romans 10:17, read Revelation 1:3, study Acts 17:11, memorize Psalm 119:9-11, and meditate on Psalm 1:2-3.

The Word of God ministered in our hearts by the Holy Spirit is the only power on earth that can transform us from worldliness to true spirituality. It is all we need to be made "complete, thoroughly equipped for every good work" (2 Timothy 3:16, NKJV). We will be *"able to test and approve God's will—his good, pleasing and perfect will"* (Romans 12:2b). It is the will of God for every believer to be a living sacrifice for Jesus Christ.

- **1 Corinthians 6:20 KJV**

  For ye are bought with a price: therefore, glorify God in your body and spirit, which is God's.

As a living sacrifice, we must come to God willingly, accepting that He is our Father and is due honor because His grace and mercy allow us to live our lives under a free will covenant.

- **Acts 17:28 KJV**

  In him, we live, move, and have our being; as your poets have said, we are also his offspring.

We are indeed the children of God and should willingly sacrifice ourselves to glorify and worship the creator of our very existence. The one who provided everything in our lives from the beginning of time.

Chapter 12

One Christ, One Body, Jesus is Lord

One Christ

Given that the Bible is the inspired written word of God, I wanted to include some scripture that confirms it for those who might have doubts. However, I have always had the understanding that God doesn't need me to prove His existence. I have a friend who was an atheist when we met. He would constantly want to challenge me regarding anything I would say that had any spiritual context. At first, I just ignored him; but after realizing his goal was to prove me wrong about anything that might represent God, I decided to say whatever came to mind knowing that he was going to look it up to come back and tell me how wrong I was. After a few months of attempting to counter everything, he came to me one day and said he had decided to accept Jesus as his Lord and Savior because he couldn't dispute God's word. It's been several years since that happened, but he is still saved and leading a righteous life. I didn't have to convince him because through his research he convinced himself. I chose not to argue or enter into debates because no matter what he thought, I've learned to stand firmly on the word of God. I only share this story because God doesn't need our defense. It's more likely that those who read, and study God's word will inevitably teach themselves by sowing the seeds of the word into themselves, even if it is unintentional. As previously stated, the word of God is a living word, and it works.

There is "One Christ." He is the only bridge to cover the gap of sin between God and man. The following scriptures provide a better understanding of why we know there is only "One Christ."

> **2 Timothy 3:16-17**: "*All Scripture is God-breathed and is useful for teaching, rebuking, correcting, and training in righteousness, so that the servant of God may be thoroughly equipped for every good work.*"
>
> **Isaiah 9:6** "*For unto us a child is born, unto us a son, is given: and the government shall be upon his shoulder: and his name shall be called 'Wonderful, Counsellor, The mighty God, The everlasting Father, The Prince of Peace.*"
>
> **John 10:30** Jesus said: "My Father and I are one."
>
> **Matthew 1:23** "*Behold, a virgin shall be with child and bring forth a son, and they shall call his name Emmanuel, which being interpreted is, God with us.*"
>
> **Revelation 1:8** "*I am Alpha and Omega, the beginning, and the ending, saith the Lord, which is, and which was, and which is to come, the Almighty.*"
>
> **Isaiah 7:14** "*Therefore, the Lord himself shall give you a sign; Behold, a virgin shall conceive, bear a son, and call his name Immanuel.*"

1 John 5:20 *"And we know that the Son of God is come, and hath given us an understanding, that we may know him that is true, and we are in him that is true, even in his Son Jesus Christ. This is the true God and eternal life."*

John 1:1-3 *"In the beginning, was the Word, and the Word was with God, and the Word was God. The same was at the beginning with God. All things were made by him, and without him was not anything made that was made."*

John 8:24 *"I said therefore unto you, that ye shall die in your sins: for if ye believe not that I am he, ye shall die in your sins."*

John 1:14 *"And the Word was made flesh, and dwelt among us, (and we beheld his glory, the glory as of the only begotten of the Father,) full of grace and truth."*

1 Corinthians 8:6 '*But to us there is but one God, the Father, of whom are all things, and we in him; and one Lord Jesus Christ, by whom are all things, and we by him*".

John 3:16-17 One Christ (and only One).

"For God so loved the world, that he gave his only Son, that whoever believes in him should not perish but have eternal life. For God did not send his Son into the world to condemn the world, but so that the world might be saved through him."

One Body:

1 Corinthians 12: 12-13 (KJV)

> *"For as the body is one, and hath many members, and all the members of that one body, being many, are one body: so also, is Christ. For by one Spirit are we all baptized into one body, whether we be Jews or Gentiles, whether we be bond or free; and have been all made to drink into one Spirit."*

In Matthew 16:15-18 Jesus asked the disciples: "Who say ye that I am?" Simon Peter answered and said, "you are the Son of the living God." Pleased with the answer Peter gave to his question and, referring to it as a "divine intervention," Jesus stated, And I also say unto thee, *"Thou art Peter, and upon this rock, I will build my church; and the gates of hell shall not prevail against it."*

It should be noted that Jesus said, I will build "my church" (singular tense). That implies one church, worldwide, and working together as one unit. His statement is not a reflection of division or separatism of any kind. It's about the unity of humankind as expected within a single body by God Almighty. There is no room for anything less than unity if we are to be in Christ. The only opinion that should matter is God's. We should also understand that in the same manner as the human body can function through its coordinated efforts, each member supporting the Body of Christ should operate under the God-given influence of the Holy Spirit as One. It is vital to use the gifts provided to govern the actions that will accomplish God's desire that none should perish by spreading the gospel with the talent(s) we've been given.

There is a place for everyone in the Body of Christ. And, given that we are winners through Christ Jesus, and, more than conquerors through Him that loved us, we will know that we can do all things through Christ who strengthens us. It doesn't matter what culture, color, age differences, personal likes, or dislikes; nothing matters other than the fact that we are to love everyone. Scripture teaches us that: "Above all, *love each other deeply because love covers over a multitude of sins.*" (1 Peter 4:8) *"My command is this: Love each other as I have loved you."* (John 15:17) *"And now these three remain faith, hope, and love. But the greatest of these is love."* (1 Corinthians 13:13) Numerous scriptures in the Bible command us to love each other; therefore, God's expectation within the Body of Christ is undeniable. In addition, God also commands us to love our enemies. In Matthew 5:44, Jesus says: *"But I say unto you, love your enemies, bless them that curse you, do good to them that hate you, and pray for them which despitefully use you, and persecute you."*

That we are to love one another goes without saying. Is it easy? Not at all. However, every effort should be made to make it happen. In reality, it's actually "fighting the good fight of faith," which we are commanded to do by our Lord.

Jesus is Lord

For Jesus to be our Savior, we must accept the authority that comes with Him being our Lord. It is He that provides the directions in life that we are to follow along the path of righteousness. If He is not given complete control of our lives, He cannot be our Savior. And yes, indeed, God's grace and mercy endure forever; but when we, by our own free will, which has been gifted to us, do not honor our agreement by putting our best foot forward, the outcome is a failure. There is absolutely no way that Jesus can be our Savior without being our Lord. Concerning God's grace and mercy, it's been demonstrated repeatedly, again and again. There will be times that we fail in our attempt to live righteously. God already knew it could and would happen, so He provided a graceful way for us to get back on the right track and that is through the act of us asking for forgiveness. The formula for this is demonstrated in Matthew 18: 21-22. When Peter came to Jesus and asked, “Lord, how often shall I forgive my brother or sister who sins against me? Up to seven times?” Jesus answered, “I tell you, not seven times, but seven times seventy.”

We’re commanded to be holy because God is holy, and He gives us every opportunity to walk the path of righteousness willingly. He gave the life of His very own Son so that we might be saved, and that alone makes Him worthy to be our Lord. Therefore, we are blessed to have Him as our Savior.

> **Philippians 2:9-11** (NKJV): *“Therefore God also has highly exalted Him and given Him the name, which is above every name, that at the name of Jesus every knee should bow, of those in heaven, and those on earth, and of those under the earth, and that every tongue should confess to the glory of God the Father.”*

Chapter 13

DEAD OR ALIVE

During various stages of this book, I've talked about "free will." In this final chapter, I want to ensure that my readers have as much of a clear understanding as I can provide.

Ecclesiastics 3:1-8 tells us this: *"There is a time to live and a time to die. A time to plant and a time to harvest."* I want to assure you that the time to plant is now while we are still upright, breathing, and alive. The free will that has been given to us by God has an end time. That time is when we meet death. Until then, we need to plant seeds to bring a fruitful harvest. The most important seed that we can plant is a "seed of faith" by accepting Jesus as our Lord and Savior. It's more than just saying it from your mouth. That's just the beginning. You have to build it in your heart. Proverbs 4:23 says that we are to *"Keep our hearts with all diligence."* Since God looks at the heart rather than the mind for the truth in us, we should always, continually, and carefully weigh the content of our hearts to make certain it remains pure. This requires us to constantly be on guard to keep a pure and clean heart, allowing God to search it and reveal to us any seeds of evil forming within. Prayer and reading our Bible enable us to keep a rein on our hearts. These are the greatest weapons of spiritual warfare that God has given us.

As indicated earlier, we will all meet death one day. When that happens, the consequences or our life's decision to accept or deny Jesus as our Lord and Savior will be our ticket into a new and eternal life. It will be too late to change our minds at that point. We will either enter the Gates of Heaven or the Gates of Hell. Both will be for eternity. The word of God is very clear. What does God say about hell?

In Matthew 13:42, Jesus says: *"And shall cast them into a furnace of fire: there shall be wailing and gnashing of teeth."*

Hell, like Heaven, is never ending; however, you must ask yourself if you want the constant never-ending horrors of Hell or if you want to enter through the Gates of Heaven, where you will be enveloped in the presence of Almighty God, free from sin and the evils of this world.

An eternal dwelling place where everything works according to the will of God.

The choice is ours. If you have not already accepted Jesus as your Lord and Savior, I encourage you to do so before it is too late. All you have to do is say this prayer and mean it in your heart, and Jesus will do the rest:

Jesus, I believe you are the Son of God, that you died on the cross to rescue me from sin and death and to restore me to the Father. I now choose to turn from my sins, self-centeredness, and every part of my life that does not please you. I choose you. I give myself to you. I receive your forgiveness and ask you to take your rightful place in my life as my Lord and Savior. Come reign in my heart, fill me with your love and your life, and help me become a truly loving person—a person like you. Restore me, Jesus. Live in me. Love through me. Thank you, God. In Jesus' name, I pray. Amen.

You have been accepted if you said this prayer and meant it in your heart. Please read your Bible, find a good church home, and meditate daily on God's word. His assurance is that He will never leave, forsake, or fail you. Amen and Amen!!!

CPSIA information can be obtained
at www.ICGtesting.com
Printed in the USA
BVHW061046151222
654216BV00010B/749